Signs of a Poetic Life

Catharine Steinberg

Signs of a Poetic Life

A selection of poems

Acknowledgements

I wish to acknowledge my deep love and gratitude for my husband
Adam. Thank you for your belief in me.

Thank you to our son Daniel and his partner Amanda,
who are enthusiastic about everything I do.

Thank you to our daughter Gillian
for her kindred poetic and artistic spirit.

Thank you to our daughter Helen,
whose love of English literature has inspired me.

Thank you to my parents, Francis and Patricia.

Finally thank you to Dr Shahid Najeeb,
who has assisted me in discovering a poetic life
and in rediscovering my love for art.

This book of poems is dedicated to my husband Adam,
and our three dear children.

Signs of a Poetic Life: A selection of poems
ISBN 978 1 76041 464 1
Copyright © text Catharine Steinberg 2017
Cover photograph: Catharine Steinberg

First published 2017 by
GINNINDERRA PRESS
PO Box 3461 Port Adelaide 5015 Australia
www.ginninderrapress.com.au

Contents

Transit of Venus	7
The Morning Fox	8
Fragments of the Wedding	9
This Garden	10
Reflections	12
The Old Land	13
The Mountain's Song	14
Time Stands Still Under the Egret Tree	15
The Small House Waits On a Cliff	16
A Song of War From the Fathomless Deep	17
The Winged House In a Storm	18
The Gallant Armada	19
The Birds and the Bees	20
Massey Estate	22
Associations To Light	23
The Meadow Dream	24
The Windy Beach Walk	26
Wisdom of the Pearl Is Music	28
The Wind Down	30
The Quiet Place	31
Lost In California	32
Nightly Creatures	33
Where the New Day Begins	34
The Graveyard In My Mind Field	35
The Profound Loss of the Child	36
The Big Tree's Final Dream	37
Bedrock and Rock-a-bye Baby	38
Cruelty	39
Heron's Joy	40
Secrets of the Bridal Oak	42

The Rain Comes	44
The Appearance of the Door	45
The Dawn Swim	46
You Have a Deadline	47
The Horses That Saved Me	48
The Alone Place	49
A Lack of Understanding	50
View From a Hilltop	52
The Casket Flowers	53
My Children	54
The Homing Pigeon	55
The Stillborn	56
The Snow White Child	58
Two Birds On an Endless Ocean	59
Patience and Running Away	61
Folding Things Up	62
Some Grief	63
Stay With Me	64
The Hidden Gem	65
The Gravedigger	66
Moongate Wedding	67
My Travels	68
Murmurings	69
Fallen Angel	71
Christmas Day 2016	72

Transit of Venus

The full moon rides high on the crest of the king tide.
Waves lip black liquid onto shore in silvery light.
The orb shines pearly and contains therein,
A mother's milky cornucopia, a suckling infant,
Man and woman in a lover's dance.

Pulsating stars, distant constellations
Have brought me here to be with you, my gentle dove.
Ancient dreams have filled my sleepy slumbers
With a trillion flickering moments of our love.
Before death's wave returns, and life is done.

The Morning Fox

I awake.
Yet a fox still lingers in morning field.
Silence cracks glassy, early light.
Mist muffled, pregnant pause.

He sits alone on frost crisp, dewy grass,
Shimmering tawny coat, white breast,
Lean limbed, enfolded in soft cosy fur.

Weak winter sun gleams in clear wild eyes,
Damp nose sniffs, black whiskers tremble.
Pant, puff, pink tongue, smile of small sharp teeth.

Shrill cry rips up the air, boom beat of wings,
Hawk high up, alarm bell peels.
Sudden red streak with white tail tip.

Mist rolls over a warm vacant shadow.
Silence cracks cold dawn light.
The dream has fled.

Fragments of the Wedding

The night is ebony breathless
And Milky Way just out of reach
Frogs croak tired little ditties
To their lovers down by the creek.

Sun and earth have it at dawn
That the rooster reigns supreme.
The sun slowly rises forlornly…then he booms

Noon bride in a moonbeam walks quietly,
In lush green of spring laden garden,
Alone with her thoughts and her flowers.

Bridesmaids in dark rose, silk, and
Organza, prance like pretty young fillies,
Heels deep in rain soaked soil.

The groom resplendent awaits,
For his love and her hand to take,
And marry midst laughter and tears.

The night is ebony breathless
And Milky Way just out of reach
Frogs croak tired little ditties
To their lovers down by the creek.

Sun and earth now have it at dawn
That the groom and his bride reign supreme.
The son rises to his beloved…then he booms!

This Garden

The garden on this side of the orchard wall is in decay and suffering badly from neglect.
But perhaps in this autumnal wilderness, rack and ruin are when life is at its joyous best.
Here the trees now overspent, groan under an excess of riotous, abundant late summer growth.
Dying sunlight glints in dappled shafts of patterned light through groves of ancient, hardy oaks.
Dust motes circle in yellow wooded hollows, caught up in swirling chaos of tiny flying creatures.
Profusion of small, white cyclamens dance under heavy, sagging boughs of weighty evergreen.
A last late summer bee, drunken, gorging, stumbles over blood red, blown roses.
Shufflings in leafy undergrowth, tell of sleepy, prickly hedgehog, hungry mouse and watchful beaky bird.
The old orchard door still stands erect, silent, shut, with peeling paint, and rusted broken hinges.
Ancient guardian of the locked forgotten world, of an old man and his faithful dog.
Hidden by verdant ivy, rotted through by moist growths of fungi, and eaten by white ant.
It once swung open into an enchanted place of gooseberries, gnarled apple trees, lazy days and gentle summer rain.
There is still a sense of hazy sleepy slumber, but beneath this heavy weight lies a feeling of something less substantial.

An eternal rest that doesn't end and the cruelty of winter's coldness is already in my bones.
The birds have flown and hardy creatures left behind scuttle to store their larders before the coming harshness.
My garden is dying and dear old orchard begs me to enter.

Reflections

Oozy meadows, brooding shadows, soft warm light.
Gentle windy breath scudding over bog black lake.
High swept clouds and immensity of sky powder blue.
Burbling brook a constant internal conversation
With itself, of past lives and thoughts about the future.
Quiet gentle grove of whispering autumn oaks.

Out here a stark beauty, wildness quite different from,
Late summer city gardens with massive overgrowth.
Up here the air is clear and heady, distance far.
Nature is lean and brown in clean, moulded, round
Wicklow hills. There is a certainty in length of things.
The shortening days and coming of the winter sun.

The Old Land

Yellow leaves on old oaks
Drooping into mossy pond.
Peat bog and orange bracken
Finished heather and prickly gorse.
Pant up the hill with stumble stones,
Hot brow and reddened cheeks.

Secret stream whispering
Through lichened rocks.
Crows cawing, flapping high up
On the hill over a kill.
A lot of deer in that wood!

Black deep lake, a gentle breeze,
Secret hollow, lonely house.
A quiet forest that has an ancient feel,
Yet somehow something different.
A land that I love, where I could live,
But what's missing is my will.

The Mountain's Song

The massive mountain towers above the lake,
Cold icy wind and cliff's sharp edge cut marrow.
The endless halt of time frozen solid.

An effigy in the brown heartless earth,
Where no soft indent of a small warm body
Can find a comfort cleft, nor sanctuary.
An endless plain, the withering vastness of it all.

My eyes lift again to the jagged mountain top,
Her deathly grip on me hidden in a mantle
Of impressionable pure white silken snow.
A singular cloud whipped disc-like at her crown.

But hear! Small gurgle of a stream not frozen over,
And silence broken by an eagle's cry.
And see! A small green bud between the rubbled stones.
There is life, and a kind of melting sadness in my soul.

Time Stands Still Under the Egret Tree

The egrets settle like flotsam in the old fig tree.
Twilight hums as the honking geese flap down
To their noisy beds, by the knobbly careworn roots.

Crickets chirrup as the quiet woman and land boys sit
And sip the quenching beers of strange feelings,
In the magic shadows beneath the dreaming tree.

Time hovers over a languid moon in the silvery pond,
As the Milky Way sways up brilliantly into indigo sky.

There is the soft lilt of light happiness in her voice,
And tinkle of laughter stirring from the dim sad past.
A sense of reaching something peaceful deep inside.

Yesterday is sure to come, tomorrow has been here too,
And the present repeats over and over to the beat of life.
I feel her new found joy in my heart and time stands still,

And I pray that the moment never ends.

The Small House Waits On a Cliff

The small house gazes blindly out with leaden glass eyes,
On the wild scene below of grey sea and darkening skies.

Alone the house stands, shuddering, yet strong,
Relentlessly buffered by spectacular storms,
The peeled ruin of a sighing, biting north wind.

But who is she at the window watching the scudding clouds,
Waiting for the endless tide's shallow turn and return,
To the quiet of a village, and the melancholic muddy harbour?

Who is she that hears the silent sorrows of men out in boats
And visits the empty fish nets in their mournful hearts?
Where deathly winter flows in, drowns all and time rushes out?

Who is she that sits outside the house, blanketed, warm,
Nestled safe from the rain-racked air, snug in a dry dusty corner?

Who is she that sips cold wine from far flung oceans?
And dreams of shipwrecks and seafarers fables whispered by
The winds, and the sirens of Neptune?

Does she remember in her heart the homely place high on a
 Cliff, and the cosy worn hearth, where cold bones find peace
 Behind aged shattered shutters?

But the wind is up now and gusting about, and the day
Shuts down, quagmired in a mist of restless calamities and an
Ocean's deep chill.

Who is she that is waiting? And for whom does she wait?
She stands and turns her gaze once more to the vigil of the sea.

A Song of War From the Fathomless Deep

There is an endless roar
As the sea breathes out her song
Of war from the fathomless deep.

Who are we to stand in the way
Of her fury,
Up here in the eagles eyrie?

The wind begins to bluster and pound,
Waves hit rocks with a mighty sound.

Each shock shakes the land
As the spirit stakes out
The scene for the final stand.

Nature will not be lenient
To those who have scarred her faces
And wounded vast ocean places.

There is no more reprieve
For the Adams and Eves
Of humankind.

As we smash ourselves
To pieces,
In our own relentless tide.

The Winged House In a Storm

We hope and pray we shall see dawn the next day.
A mighty storm has hit and begins its cruel play.

The night crashes about, the gale bawls and moans
Then it screams, and a dreadful cry chills our bones.

The banshees storm from their graves and screech
Through windowpanes, and slide in via a breach.

Something below clangs and bangs in the dark.
There are soft murmuring chants, like a requiem dirge.

The winged house weeps and shivers like a lost child,
She shudders and wants to take flight from the wild.

Beneath my bed, the earth shakes and quakes,
The roof crackles and creaks, and could easily break.

A storm in one hundred, when even the bravest can freak.

The Gallant Armada

I felt the infinity of a deep swallow in the glassy green
as I trailed behind the troubled ocean today.
A huge wall of blues, impregnable and dense.

Yet I can enter its darkest watery void
with a sweep of my hand through the mirrored surface.

To descend its throat so vast and steep
that time and space recede beyond the rim.

And it's here that I wake to the sudden sting of life
as the haint blue armada drowns itself
above the spirits in the mourning tide.

The sun's life slips behind a din of crested sound
and the roar of silent heavy clouds.

I felt death today and the destruction of the sea,
till it nibbled my foot and tossed onto me, a small life form.

Tendrils armed and ready, yet so fragile without a bone.
A gallant blue bottle, its sail set,
to bring me back once more, to life and home.

The Birds and the Bees

The buzzing bee
Frantically flits up and down.
There is no escape,
Inside the heartless window pane.
She has a frantic desire to escape
Back to life.
A life that can be seen,
Just outside,
On the other side,
Over there.

But alas, no honeyed place,
To re-enter again.
And the murderous sun
Beats her down and down.
She is found lifeless,
On the floor in the morning.
A tiny curled body,
With wings spent, and bent.
I'm sad to see her lying there.
I could have released her,
Back into her world.

Just then my eyes
Catch a shadow.
And looking
Through the cold window pane,
I see a distant small bird
Flying low over glassy waves.
Teasing the frothing foam
With the tips of her wings.
Soaring just out of reach,
From a cold watery grave
On the edge of her outer world.

And I wonder?
Does one soul have a door
That leads to the other?
Does the stop of one heartbeat
Kindle another?
Does the bee become the bird?
Do the imprisoned become free?

Massey Estate

The sap green light inside the forest
Bursts into solar rays of raindrop
Showers. Silvery echoes, drip dropping.
The sighing and spatter, an old song
Tinkling airily of the woodland folk
Amongst the pellucidity of the silent trees.

The wind and birds are quiet and hushed
In the woods today as we walk along
Below nature's vaulted leafy dome.
A temple of homage to earthly beauty,
Hellfire club and ancient burial site.
Now silent and deeply interred within
The minds of dead men and history.

Black mangled earth soggy, slosh, suck
and sinking beneath my returning feet.
Muddy wet dogs with blackened bellies
Slobbering through the churning mire,
Like sheep. Sharp words to stay on track.
And scrabbling over a babbling brook,
Mossy rocks, a slip then stumbling leap.
The slush of sodden, slithery, wet ooze.
And crackle crunch of leaf litter beneath
This canopy of sentient fir and beech.

I drink in through my senses and move on.

Associations To Light

Flickering, blinking, light, mayflies, wasn't that my speech?
 Only you used fireflies.
Light can be a wave or particular.
                      Depending on how you look at it.
Or here! You can see it through this portal or there through a Kaleidoscope.
You can't have the light without the dark.
                      In every painting or photo there has to be
The Dark... You Know.

'It's Darking, Mummy' my little child said and cried.
Oh how I ache!

But perhaps our minds are joined, yours and mine.
Light and dark, the blind leading the blind.
I can read through your eyes though mine are blind.

My mind, my ideas, associations, rich soil.
I should write. I have something to say!

The animals, creatures with their deep, sharp eyes and
Knowing ways. They know, They Know.

The Meadow Dream

I am the horse in harness
Dreaming about the meadow.
I wish that I am the horse
In the meadow in the dream.
I can only imagine a sudden hush,
Nightfall, quiet twitterings
Of insects and birds. A flutter
And strange calm all at once.

The silvery moonlight casting
Pearly spidery spells all round.
Forest animals settling down
To sleep 'Perchance to dream…'*
Of a timelessness.
Another fantasy world.
Strangeness of a nowhere space
That feels like the right place,
That feels like home.

I have lost the sense of time.
My animal body can feel time,
But only my harnessed self
Knows how to tell the time.
Now and then I miss a beat
And wish for timelessness.
It feels light, but restrictions
Abound and I am tied down…again.

I have a universe inside my mind
Bewildering unknown lands.
But where do I go to find me?
Must I go to that bewitching
Place alone to find just me?
I might discover other me's.
But where would I be
Without you to guide me?
And all this time my right hand
Has been blind to the left yet
They hold each other together.

Perhaps I am multiple?
Who knows?
What a funny thing I am!
But anyway! Just for today
I am the horse in harness
And tonight I am the horse
In the meadow in the dream.
Thank you for taking me there
And showing me where I exist.

* from *Hamlet* by William Shakespeare

The Windy Beach Walk

The beach was windy today.
Warm sun played with gusty puffs,
Buffeting my skin.
Shirt sails up, and I laugh out loud
As strangers walk by.
What was revealed about me?

Hat held down still bashing against my face,
Flapping like a trapped winged bird.
Sandals held firmly in one hand and
Sandy crunches between white crinkled toes.
I wonder if my legs look pale as the young woman
Daintily revealed just over there?
Her skin thin, and translucent as the moon.

The waves gurgle up and drown my feet,
Slopping wet and glassy against old trousers.
A slight faintness, light-headedness overcomes me
In the bright beach light.
A murmuring, a steady whispered intensity.
A child's call, the heartbeat boom of the wide blue ocean
And all sound drowned down.

The sea is careless and cool,
Dancing all around with slight shocks before retreating
Only to resist the tug back and plummet forward again.
The ceaseless shimmering tide, the push and pull
The yin and yang the universal seesaw.
The balance of life and death.

Wild thoughts, as legs strike out
And sink in the wet wake.
I wonder if there are fish just there and over there?

And he strides out ahead boldly.
Clothes fluttering, silent now.
A world away in his thoughts.
The steady beat of his kind heart
And mindful whisperings.

A dead seabird, finished above the tideline.
I wonder how far it has travelled in life
Only to lie lonely in the silent slumber of death?
And I'm on this side of life
On this side of the tide.
The great Australian dream and soul of things
Found on a windy beach one day in spring.

Wisdom of the Pearl Is Music

A grain of truth is the pearl of wisdom,
Purity lies in a musical note.
The perfection of a lingering moment
Like a drop of water suspended
In the space behind closed eyes.

The head is the point of acoustics
At the centre of a known universe.
I exist at the axis of sound that
Falls from watery instruments
Like music in a spherical round.

Pearls flow from a fountain of
Bubbles, in streams and rivulets
Spraying. Leaping over gullies
And gorges, sluicing through culverts
And tinkling in sink holes and streams.

Water wallows in cisterns and aquifers,
Cascades fall through stark wild valleys.
Winter melt roars from high bursting banks,
Foaming torrents race screaming at last
To the arms of the wide open sea.
A lonely echo whispers quietly at source
With a hush trickle of the small drip, drop.

Silver moonlight reflects on black ocean.
Butterflies pale in the soft Luna glow,
A globulous globe that trembles over
Pungent petals of waxy white flowers.
A light shower sprinkles dark leaves
With a pitter-patter and splatter-tatter.
A gentle breeze kisses air with a sigh.

The moment of life has just passed.
Before the finger lifts off the key,
Before the conductor's baton is lowered,
Before the singer has sung her last song
And before the maestro takes his bow.

Perfection is purity of sound.
One note lives but a moment and
A grain of truth exists in that pearl.
Herein lies the wisdom and truth.
That life lingers within a small grain
And the pearl at its heart is the sound.

The Wind Down

The wind down is a deep ravine of compounding turmoil.
When you think it will end it goes on and on and on.
Interminably.

The ending is never the ending until the last ounce
The last squeezed drop has been extracted
As payment for being born and living and everything.

And you are finally left as a curled up shrivelled flake
In the corner of nowhere naked and drained of
What was once the semblance of something human.

And so a numbness creeps over all the once promised land.
Forgetting swoops down in an eagle's thunderous way,
Into the deep crevasse of sorrow.

There is no possibility of a return fare on the midnight train
To stark oblivion tonight.
There are no words to describe the dying of my love for you.

The Quiet Place

Freshly mown grass dewy all day over the softness
And bouncy green density where the insects creep in.

Solitary solitude among the brambles that catch
Snag and snare. Gossamer and scarlet fuchsia heads
Hang shamelessly against the dark green foliage.
A small trifling triumph. Carpets of goblet cyclamen
Waxy petals in shady shades of lilac and white.

Woods thick with thicket and ivy, an old cedar
Choked below. Its dark dead wood clawing and
Encircling empty air in a desperation of embraces,
As if drowning in the pool of insect laden noontime.

A life and a death so close together. And yet there's
A kind of lazy watching and listening here in the quiet
As in no other place. The way of feelings that burst.
A birthing of fantasy, flickering to a burgeoning of thoughts.

Here, a back road to the life of the fairies and the fox.
All hidden and yet little spyings around a leaf here
And there a remnant of the wispy phantom disturbed.
Like a disremembered dream of the garden wanderer,
Wandering with a lost feeling, confusion and an old ache.

A sadness behind the eyes in the knowing knowledge
That what is gone is gone and what is to come will come
And sweep away this old world with one fell swoop.

Lost In California

Small town pretty America squirrels birds quiet and white.
Shimmering trees in the park scratchings scuttling and chirps.

Sweet kids, chickens and dog. An organic perfect life.
A far cry from my world and undercurrents of a felt scream.

Signs of ageing and inexorable loneliness a withheld sigh.
Night train sirens and polite dismissals of 'Why don't you…?'

Maypoles floral crowns folks dancing a foreign pagan ritual.
Cool dappled light under tender spring trees. Budding delayed.

A market blanketed by heat, the desire to run away.
Flat horizons by the road and fruit trees in endless deadly rows.

Pink dusty twilight hangs over brooding silent orchards, and
Distant light fades under branches as the car winds slowly home.

The crop duster is a scourge of this promised but scoured land.
Vague reminiscences of a murder movie like hex and hillbilly.

Strange dreams of a couch, and a key that doesn't lock.
Another of shameless abandonment and heady sexual pleasures.

Then I thirst for water in a waterless landscape in a dusty plain.
For hours we career around the flat lands of a wire-scape city.

Hispanics here service the over-wealthy of the big Americanos,
In a country of rifle-clutching civil rights and only a lucky few.

Beggars in ragged millions encroach on me with plaintive cries.
I long for my big red land, home and the silence of the room.

Nightly Creatures

The white owl hovers in the gloaming.
A secret nightly soul, a dream remnant.
The flitter of a being at the edge of light.
The mist rolls in and fantasy flies in a ring
From the halo of the moon.

There is an inhalation deep into the chasm
Of the throat, and tidal respiration of my sea.
The ocean of straw fluid and blood churn
Ceaselessly from my faithful heart after all
These many long long years.

The owl glides. Muffled hooves thud dully
On steamy pastures of grey green tendrils.
A tossed black mane gentle eyes.
Dark wild spirit watches me knowingly, silent.
A basket woven of dreams, bright stones
Glinting, fiery stardust from the rim of thought.

The morning comes and shadows slip away.
A faint bird call and chorus of beaky chatterers
Crescendo. The snored cacophony halts
Coughs clear. The daylight eyes blink open
While others droopy close.

Sunny warmth zooms loudly through cold glass.
Cool forgetful air feels like oozy treacle between
The pores of day.
The nightly owl, dark horse, the weaver's basket
Of dreamer's dreams and starry stones have gone.

Where the New Day Begins

Did you know?

The birth of a new day begins in utter darkness,
At the stroke of midnight where old days go to die
In the hollowed-out soul, right here.

Time begins, at the core of deep blackness.
Pale shapes emerge. A flicker of thought.
New dawn. A longed for light.

Change begins in a land of despair where old ghosts
Wait with hungry mouths to swallow you down.
Yet you, the remains of a fragile shattered fragment,
Hang on through endless night. A tiny sliver of hope.
To reach the startle of another morning birthday.

The Graveyard In My Mind Field

There exists in my mind field a graveyard.
Where my sadness and mourning lie buried.
I go there sometimes to weep.

This dark place lies deep within me.
And only I know where it is hidden.
I am the keeper of death for those who lie therein.

The ghosts of children and adults gather.
The crowds smile and echo my tears.
Ephemeral waifs lost to life for years.

They have no memory of me.
Nor that I strived to keep them in life.
But they slipped away from my grasp.

There exists in my mind field a graveyard.
Where my sadness and mourning lie buried.
I go there sometimes to weep.

The Profound Loss of the Child

He got lost somewhere between this world and *in utero*.
No one picked him up gave him form, a sense of self.
There was no, 'Who am I?'
There *was* no *who*, no *am*, no *I*.
There *was* 'I'm feeling a little better this week'.
But *who* was he? No one knew, not he, not me.
So *who* was feeling a little better each week?

You may well ask.

The Big Tree's Final Dream

They were killing the big old tree all day.
It didn't seem right, such a proud being.
The wood was sound and solid with sap.
Groans from the saw, the power of the tool.

Small men steal a dream, and vanquish.

I float above the lake leaning over the side
Gazing into the transparent depth, flying over
As the sturdy oars dip and glide dip and glide.
In the vortex of deep water endless eddies swirl.

Dragging me down and down and down…

The moans just a whisper a fading jaded sigh
On the wind as it sheers the cold glassy surface.
The tree is the boy, the boat, the lake, a wish.
Then it is gone, the boat, the lake, the dream.

I the tree want to live.
But I found myself too late.

Bedrock and Rock-a-bye Baby

Bedrock and rock-a-bye baby,
In the cradle that rickety rocks.
The bedrock of man's civilisation
Is off kilter and crashed on the rocks.
The screech of plastic toy lullaby's
Mindless games on psychotic screens.
The wipe out of a child's own play
By technology on endless display.
What has happened to rock-a-bye baby?
What madness have we grown up in?
What bedrock have we forgotten?

Cruelty

Create anew,
The instructions tell me.
Yes create renew
Twist life by the throat
And he is sent bawling
Into the world of thought
Daydreams and yes, terror.
Is this the price
We pay for life, a moment?
And whom may I ask
Is rewarded for the privilege?
Whoever thought this was fun
Is cruel beyond belief.

Heron's Joy

I remember this day immortal in my keep-safe.
Wind soughing ever restless over choppy water.
Shimmering sea haze cool spray.
Voices faint, swept away by the intruding immediacy
Of light and the sound of a deep ocean boom.
Dizzy exaltation, goosebumps on excited skin
Still sandy scratchy and scoured.
White boat, a dot lost on turquoise reef
For turtles rays and sharks to seek.

Flippers, life jackets, goggles, snorkels.
Snuffles, wet nose, sweet saliva in salty throat.
Staying close to the boat floating over reef
I watch water ripples rumpled up by wind.
And looking down through clear crystal water
To a shadowy world of glinting coral-yellow sand,
A multitude of darting fish shapes
Sizzle in drowned sunlight enticing us to enter.

Jump in. A sharp descent enfolded
Within a shock of cool champagne and bubbly foam.
Air world narrowed to oxygen in plastic tubes.
An umbilical reminder of landlocked creaturehood.
Sudden muffled roaring sound in ears.
Each breathe and heartbeat reverberates through bone,
Certain signs of inner life
And sentinel reminders of fragile tenuous mortality.

My children swim. Big windmill arms and
Vigorous beating kicks over beckoning reef.
My flippers give me strength and jacket buoys me up.
Sun flickers warmth upon my back.
The children dive deep down to explore fishy treasures,
I watch above afloat afraid to follow.
Sweet young ones glide below. Limbs beating,
Twisting, circling. A mermaid flying down and down.

Sunlight glances bent through green glassy water
On tanned skin. Swimsuits coral-coloured
With wavy frills, shine on girlie cheeky bottoms.
Young boy-man swims, slim and seal-slick sleek.
Long brown hair trails in seaweed pearly bubbles.
They swim free and careless curious and joyful in play.
A silent song like sirens deep within
The watery liquor of the Earth's oceanic womb.

Secrets of the Bridal Oak

The oak she stands broad and grand,
Rustling her new mantle in the park.
The last of her kind in these antipodean climes,
And forgotten here today.
Her big boughs sag heavy and curve down
To the ground full-breasted.
Clothed in kaleidoscopic green silky leaves,
The bridal gown of early spring.
Deep down her pale limbs settle
Into buried dark and cool artesian streams.
Sipping rich moisture ever upwards
In fanning veins to tiny velvet twigs.
As many roots plunge far below
As branches are above.
A close union of two halves
Split from a single acorn.
She grows up to gild the sun
Whilst her sister delves in dense black earth.
Each a shared, beloved, whole.
Married for life, and yet not spouse,
Abundant seeds but no children tomorrow.
I walk below her sap laden, leafy canopy
And drink in her finery and glory.
There is a hush, and hardly a breeze
To stir her fine new gossamer veils.
The sun glimmers through her shadows.
A dreamy moment passes and
She seems to shake her tinkling head.

Alas, no groom in this big red land,
Just a bride of great voluptuous beauty,
Unseen unheard in fulsome flower.
But then I see a kookaburra seated neatly on her arm,
And gazing Oh! So quietly back at me.
His silent wise eyes tell me the secrets of his tree.

The Rain Comes

In the quiet of an unrisen morning,
Rain comes in big drops.
I snuggle down in bed and listen,
To the sudden wet squall
And birds taking fright.

Limp green foliage
And petals are washed anew.
Balm after hottest days.
The earth's sweet cool elixir
Of vital life.

Mother Nature refreshes
Wasted dried out land, and rivers flow.
The forest will soon roar her songs again.
A time for joy and play.

I lie dreaming of the quiet pitter-patter rain
Here inside my head.
The crunchy squelch and splatter
Of tiny raindrops into thoughts.

The Appearance of the Door

I swear it wasn't there before
Though I have come four years or more.
Each time I entered through the hall
There was no door but empty wall.

Then all at once as clear as day
It gleamed so bright and freshly dreamed.
I'm confused! How could I not have seen
The door that's always beckoned me?

I have searched so very long
For missing pieces, for memory lost.
You said, 'Please take a look, right there.'
I was blind and answered, 'Where?'

I'm still unsure it's real and think
It's a trick of the eye or a kind of trap.
How long has my mind been in dark night
To something clear and in plain sight?

The Dawn Swim

This morning,
I went for a solitary dawn swim.
It was there that I saw
The silent white nightly creature.
He crouched there quietly
As I swam to the end.
My presence unknown.
Both caught in our reveries
Of the ending night
The finishing of timeless dreaming.

He seemed surprised as I rose
Through the aqueous surface.
A strange naked land creature
Filmed in glassy liquid.
Not dried out by harsh daylight to come
Nor wounds yet visible on pale skin.
He uttered a small hesitant 'Meow'
And moved along on his fluffy way.
Out of sight now but still held in mind
For a lingering twilight second.

You Have a Deadline

You have a deadline.
I heard a voice say in my head tonight.
So I will steal the key and take it back with me.
To remember in a sad old clutching way
Where my heart lies and where you lay.

There is no going back no more. Time lost.
To find again the path to find your door.
No way to make order of my own chaos.

Too late to find the forbidden trail
That leads to your soul now old and frail.
It is locked and you are forever to be,
A familiar unknown stranger to me.
All that remains is this rusted key
That I will now carry away with me.

The Horses That Saved Me

Soft fur large warm familiar body.
Sweaty smell dusty comfort.
Soft muzzle nuzzle warm snuffles
And breathe in my hair.
Brown eyes that reflect
A universe and my soul in it.

Oh, how I loved you!
You were there to save me
When my kind couldn't bear me
Didn't want me, cast me off.
I just want to be with you
And run free with you.
No more caring
Just a wild spirit and just in you.

The Alone Place

There is a cold and dreary place
Where I go on alone.
Deep into the grief ravine
That chills me to my bones.
Back through the vales of time
And lost mists of misery.
Where memory lies misshapen
In hard and frosted ground.
The path leads there, way down
To caverns of black despair.
A shadowy swamp that's all consumed
Choked and overgrown.
Again I fear to tread there
To waken souls from ages past,
Or hush the anguished crying
Of a young child abandoned, lost.
This is a cold and perilous trek
In the slippery dark abyss.
A silent place where I go on alone
All by my weary self.
The gate is reached the handle turns
I step in through the gap.
Ghosts rise up fill me with dread
And the urge to run back up.

A Lack of Understanding

What is it that I don't understand
About the mother leopard
Who devours her own dead cub?
And why does she utter wretched grieving cries?
Is she still a loving mother calling for
Her lost baby in the fading African light?

Or is this blind savagery, primitive instinct
An ancient animal ritual?
A dim perception of taking back inside
What grew in her, was born from her
Of her body, but from the other side?

Is this a meal for life and hope of rebirth?
And that she ate her baby out of love
To will him back to her before the
Last lingering smell of his little soul
Departs in darkest night?
To curl him up deep inside and keep him
Safe and snug next to her beating heart?
A kind of remembering, in a sad way?

But the mournful growls fill up the air
That carries her plaintiff yearning
To hear a single tiny echo
An endearing last meow.
But no more me and thou
No more here and now
Nor the presence of a small cuddly body
That brought her joy outside her own.

It seems to me there is no line drawn here
Between love and hate, just life and death
And what death does to life, and to a mother's love.

View From a Hilltop

Seated on a bench in dappled shade on a hill
Faraway from the beating sun.
The day grows weary the hazy brightness
Casts mellow spells upon the land.
The southerly comes up with a kind of hush
Blowing in a billowy stream.
The trees surround me whispering
With a gentle swish and a sighing secret sound.
Field guns burst with sudden shots
That fracture air to frighten hungry birds.
The Bang! Bang! Ruptures a crackled echo
That ripples, rolling down the vale.
But birds still warble chirrup caw and tinkle,
Busy in late noon light.
The dam below sings monotonous tinny tunes
Of pumps and wheezy motors.
And further on shadows grow long
Under gums and yellow paddocks.
No crickets yet venture forth to sing
For the dying of the harsh gold light.
And far away a buzzing car kicks up dirt
On a dusty dusky track.
The sun feels warm and dry on weathered skin
As I close my eyes to drink the magic in.

The Casket Flowers

The flowers are still
Arranged and spill
Over the florist's bench.

A massive petalled
Promise of abundance.
Overflowing evidence
Of a lively riotous joy.

But their life is brief
And a casket's grief
Will soon be hidden
With their sacrificial gift
As a yellow and white bouquet.

Left to wither, they will perish
In the silence of a grave.
To meet with dark and
Death eternal
Long before their time.

What cruelty is this,
That we lovingly condemn
Such a beautiful whimsy
To the enclaves of a tomb?

My Children

I don't ever want to forget
How my children look.
The familiar smells
Achingly sweet smiles
Small arms, round ears.
Warm sweaty scalps
And teary red cheeks.
Laughter and joy
Chaos and fears.
Most treasured true darlings
Of all my long years.

The Homing Pigeon

The great white bird glides silent
Dreamlike over endless seas.
Mighty roar inside massive engines,
A comfort to my ears.
Sleepless, restless, bone weary
Heavy headed, withered eyes.
I'm coming home again to you
My dearest darlings by the by.

Faithful homing pigeon
I, fly back to you
To heal my aching heart.
But strange to say, past strife
With us then splintered mine apart.
Each half was flung to farthest pole
Of earth and oceans blue.
My soul cast down in shades of grief
And all because of you.

The Stillborn

The baby was too little to survive, born before time.
And yet she drew breath. This was unexpected!
She was designated as stillborn, but compelled to live
Against the odds, by her own small beating heart.

A thin wavering cry burst from cherub lips. A chirp.
Her first and last dawn chorus before long night.
Silence filled the room. The midwives were in awe.
The audacity of this miniature human child.

Doctor please come! We are unsure what to do.
The mother is distressed. The child will live briefly.
She has become a person with inhalation of air
But death has not yet claimed her for himself.

A naked baby lies abandoned in humidicrib.
I gaze enraptured by her perfect tiny form.
Too young too small and, ah yes sure signs of death.
Pale lips, fragile chest fluttering against gravity too great.

A mother sits beside the crib, silent tired spent.
Arms and womb now hollow of immortal gift.
Have they touched? Have they even said hello?
Their cries aren't heard. They exist and die alone.

Would you like to hold your baby? She won't live.
She turns to me her sad lost eyes in silence.
The crib is opened, oxygen spent. Death so close.
At last, the small remnant of life is safe in mother's arms.

You can talk to her let her hear your voice.
They say that hearing is the last thing to go, you know.
The mother holds her dying baby close.
Love lives a moment but sorrow always lingers.
I leave the tender couple to their life.

The Snow White Child

The child's not breathing, come immediately!

Racing, stifled panic, cold dreaded and mouth dried.
Bursting into sudden clamour, noise, harsh voices,
White coats, sucking tubes, cold metal, brazen light.

A small stranger is dying in there today.

The parents are waiting here. Can you have a word?

Hello, I'm Doctor… Tell me what happened to your son?
We found him pale just lying there. We called and called.
He will be OK, doctor? There is hope in their eyes.

A choke in my throat. Please wait one moment.

The team, pump and shock the small fragile chest.
Flying hands, blood oozes, stained sheet. You're the doctor!
Make a decision! Do we stop or carry on? All eyes turn to me.

I gaze at small snow white child. Not a breathe, not a flutter.

No sign of life. Please. Stop. They stop. He dies.

I'm so very sorry but your child has just died. He didn't suffer.
Can we see him, doctor, Please? Yes, but wait please.

They still have hope in their eyes.

The dead weight of snow white child lies warmly in my arms.
His life has flown. The loving ones must say goodbye alone.
The old way.

I close the door on anguish. Wake up, son! Wake up, son!

Two Birds On an Endless Ocean

Thanks, for the sublime moments in time
The fullness the emptiness
The separateness the unity of my life.
The spaces where I can reflect with gratitude
On reality and unreality,
And to be at peace in the present.

I understand that my search for thee is right here
Where I am in this place where I exist
With thee, with others and alone.
And though I may not see nor hear thee
Or rarely feel thee, thou art present
Both inside and outside.

Nowhere and everywhere in the world
With me in my soul, yet not in me.
Thou art both near and far from me
But in close relation to me, up against me.
Within my grasp and yet not to be grasped.
Ever present in a single, twofold
And multiplicity of ways.

My suffering is to overcome myself,
And the turning away of me from thee.
To truly understand the meaning
Of us, the two birds of my existence.
And to believe in the way of my truth.

I may never fully grasp anything of thee
Or very little of I, myself at all.
But I am grateful to thee for this gift
For revealing the truth of who I am.
Being who I am in the universe and

In relation to thee.

Inspired by *I and Thou* by Martin Buber

Patience and Running Away

The act of patience
Is when the stream is bubbling underneath.
I'm writhing and squirming in silence
And all I want to do is shout and run away.

And when you say that you will miss me,
All I want to do is run away again
From the burst of fiery feelings
That run the risk of melting my heart.

I didn't realise before today that for you,
My going away feels like an eternity.
I knew what others meant when they looked sad.
But I looked the other way and didn't shout or cry.

And I ran away and I still run away.
Please be patient with me.

Folding Things Up

Fold yourself up into the quiet sleep.
I will not be going with you my dear.
Don't think I won't miss you, I will.
But I won't be looking back.

Don't fret, all will be well,
And you will find immeasurable peace.
Don't think I will be there to hold your hand.
I want to, but I'm staying here where I am.

And when they place you in the cold ground
I will be long gone back to my home.
But don't think I'll ever forget you.
I am remembering you every single day.

Some Grief

I haven't been out for a walk
In the hills this time.
The slippage seems inevitable.
There is no escape
To the green mossy open of spaces
And enfolding valley browns.

There is only an impenetrable
Lingering mist.
A suffocation.
An inside anguish of being.

Soon the deepest tears
Will leak back up
And before too long,
The time will come to pass
When once again
Summer has withered and gone.

Stay With Me

I will miss you when you've gone.
But I'm forever pulling away from you
And your eyes always search for mine.
'Stay with me' they say.

I can't and I won't.

And there is always something
That bars the way between you and me.
While I'll miss you when you've gone,
I sometimes hate it when you are here.

I do care, but the love we have is unbearable.

The Hidden Gem

Blackberries picked from the hedgerows
Pop into purple flavours
In the hungry of our mouths.
Tangy and sweet from the richness
Of sodden thick brown peat.

And a burbling brook gurgles nearby
In a hidden liquidious way,
As puddles overflow from the slanting rain
That has driven down funnelled boreens.

Summer evening sunbeams shaft
Like golden showers of afterglow
On fading electric green fields.
Dusky motes dance below shiny wet trees
In the under light, of a late autumnal day.

And the opaque and languorous moon
Lies lazy and high in the cool pale blue
Of an early September sky.

And on the way home to sleep, we creep
To steal watery plums steeped deep,
In muddy damp soil from an old orchard
With secrets and hidden gems to keep.

The Gravedigger

We wondered if he'd died
Or that something was wrong
As we drove along.

There was no answer
As we called and called.
It was odd and we fretted.

But he'd been digging a grave
For the old widow he said.
Who had passed on her way
Through the night.

'It's what the neighbours
Do for each other
Hereabouts,' he added
And nodded his head with a sigh.

He'd sat shiva with others
At her wake all night
And returned
With a hollowed out voice.

And he greeted us quietly
Still dressed in the clothes
That were caked
In the cemetery mud.

The keening and drinking
Were over he assured us.
And he was back to his self
Once again.

Moongate Wedding

While the grandparents snoozed
The lovebirds were married
In a humanist way
In front of the old Moongate.
And the rain came down
As the umbrellas went up
And the celebrant was soaked to the skin.

While the grandparents slumbered
The lovebirds, now married
In a humorous way
Moved in through the old Moongate.
And the rain dried up
As the umbrellas came down
With the celebrant still soaked to his skin.

My Travels

I have walked along this path
The whole of my life
And I carry with me many heavy objects.

I have come to a waterfall
And stop to take my rest.
I now realise that I'm looking for a village.

Murmurings

The milky air is pillowy sweet
With your quiet murmurings
In my sleepy ears.

Much kindness can be found
In strangers, in the oddest of places
And down the deepest of wells.

My thoughts poured down
As the rain splattered, tattered
Along the wrong path.

When gardenia flowers wither and die,
More buds blossom on the same bush.

The enormity of the news
That you won't be coming home
Only hits my heart much later.

The quiet trees bring me stories
With their sighs.
So much is lost in translation.

Sunlight dances recklessly
On my closed eyelids,
And the red fear becomes a reality.

The purpose of each life
Is to be a drop in the endless ocean.
Every drop contains a universal truth.

I began life as a minuscule blob
And then this happened.

I think you know what you are doing.
But to me, it feels like you are heading
Straight into oncoming traffic.

Fallen Angel

At first there came a low sigh
From over the flattened horizon.
It rose like a hollowed out whistle
Over shady and silent ravines
Travelling fast in a fiery descent.

It was the song of a falling angel
Plummeting down with burning wings.
Her cry was a broken heart yearning
For the last chance at celestial bliss
In the deepening crimson hued sky.

A mighty roar chased after steel engines
On the back of a black sonic storm.
A tumult of showering embers
Followed her sobs of faltering desires
As she got lost in the vast setting sun.

The snake girl glimmers in twilight
Like a far away mystical dream.
In a landscape of dry twisting rivers
And broken back rusty tin shacks.

Her eyes glitter with tears of promise
And the want of so many tomorrows,
That water will rain in this vast arid land.
But then she is gone with the clouds.

Christmas Day 2016

Sea urchins, molluscs,
Anemones, algae,
Necklace of seaweed
Cling to the slippery rocks.

The water gurgles up
Then circles in swirls
That slide like skin and trickle
Into twinkling pools that refresh
The places where crabs live.

And I think of how happiness
Can live for a moment
In the land of the sand
As the sun empties itself
Into this wide open space
And drenches the
hollows in my skin.

And while the salty breeze
buffets me, children rush in
With a splash and a squeal
As they delight
With a little bit of fright
The encircling embrace of the sea.

A brown dog bounds around
And is washed in a rock pool
By the woman in a red bikini,
Who smiles me a white smile
And then stops for a moment
To gaze at the shimmering horizon.

And elsewhere
The life-giving water
Lips quietly away
At the edge of the beach
And washes my feet
In a bath of bubbly foam.

I sit for a moment
To capture a dream
In the haze of the day
And the blast of the blazing sun.

www.ingramcontent.com/pod-product-compliance
Lightning Source LLC
Chambersburg PA
CBHW062153100526
44589CB00014B/1817